We hope this book has been informative and helpful on your journey to understanding and celebrating older adults. Thank you for your interest and support!

Title: Unleashing Global Cinema 1980-2000

Subtitle: A deep dive into international cinema during this period

Series: Lights, Camera, History: The Best Movies of 1980-2000

By Adriana Shannon

"A film is never really good unless the camera is an eye in the head of a poet."
Orson Welles, director and actor

"Cinema is a matter of what's in the frame and what's out."
Martin Scorsese, director

"In the movies, we are all leading lives with subtitles."
Federico Fellini, director

"The only way to do a good job is to love what you do."
Steve Jobs, former CEO of Pixar

"Film is a disease. When it infects your bloodstream, it takes over as the number one hormone; it bosses the enzymes; directs the pineal gland; plays Iago to your psyche."
Frank Capra, director

"Making movies is like being a general: You lead a group of people, and you have to be organized, and you have to make sure everyone is on the same page."
Ridley Scott, director

"Cinema is a matter of what's in the frame and what's out."
Martin Scorsese, director

"A film is never really good unless the camera is an eye in the head of a poet."
Orson Welles, director and actor

"Cinema is a language. It can say things, big and small."
David Lynch, director

"I am a storyteller. I tell stories with pictures and sound."
George Lucas, director and producer

Table of Contents

Introduction
The significance of global cinema during the period of 1980-2000

The period of 1980-2000 was a crucial time for global cinema, as it saw the emergence of a new wave of filmmakers from around the world who challenged traditional modes of filmmaking and produced groundbreaking works that captivated audiences worldwide. During this time, international auteurs like Akira Kurosawa, Wong Kar-wai, and Pedro Almodovar rose to prominence, while films such as Ran, In the Mood for Love, and All About My Mother broke new ground in terms of cinematic technique and storytelling.

The significance of global cinema during this period cannot be overstated, as it marked a major shift away from the dominance of Hollywood and towards a more diverse and vibrant world cinema. As international co-productions became more common, filmmakers from different countries began to collaborate on projects that transcended national boundaries and showcased a variety of cultural perspectives. This led to a wealth of exciting new films that explored themes such as identity, politics, and social issues in fresh and innovative ways.

One of the key factors driving this new wave of global cinema was the impact of globalization on the film industry. As new technologies and communication systems emerged, it became easier for filmmakers to connect with each other and to bring their work to a global audience. This led to a democratization of the film industry, as filmmakers from developing countries were able to access new markets and compete on a more equal footing with their Hollywood counterparts.

At the same time, global cinema during this period was not without its challenges. Many filmmakers faced censorship and political pressure in their home countries, while others struggled to find funding or to get their films distributed internationally. Despite these obstacles, however, the films of this era continue to inspire and captivate audiences to this day.

In this book, we will explore the major trends and themes in global cinema during the period of 1980-2000. We will examine the works of key filmmakers from around the world, and analyze the ways in which their films reflected and influenced the broader cultural and political context of their time. We will also interview international directors, actors, and producers who were instrumental in bringing these movies to a global audience, and discuss the lasting impact of these films on world cinema as a whole.

Join us as we embark on a journey through the world of global cinema during this exciting and transformative period, and discover how these films continue to shape our understanding of the world around us.

The major filmmakers and their works during this period

The period of 1980-2000 was a time of great creativity and innovation in global cinema, as a new generation of filmmakers emerged from around the world to challenge traditional modes of filmmaking and create groundbreaking works that captivated audiences worldwide. In this section, we will examine some of the major filmmakers of this period and their most notable works, and explore the ways in which their films reflected and influenced the broader cultural and political context of their time.

Akira Kurosawa: One of the most influential and celebrated filmmakers of this period was Akira Kurosawa, the Japanese director whose films like Ran and Dreams explored themes such as loyalty, honor, and the human condition. Kurosawa was known for his innovative use of cinematic technique, such as his use of multiple cameras and his ability to seamlessly blend genres like samurai epics and crime dramas.

Wong Kar-wai: Another major filmmaker of this period was Wong Kar-wai, the Hong Kong director whose films like Chungking Express and In the Mood for Love explored themes of love, loss, and memory. Wong was known for his use of striking visuals and music, as well as his ability to capture the mood and atmosphere of his settings in a way that was both poetic and grounded in reality.

Pedro Almodovar: In the realm of European cinema, one of the most influential filmmakers of this period was Pedro Almodovar, the Spanish director whose films like All About My Mother and Talk to Her explored themes of gender, sexuality, and identity. Almodovar was known for his bold use of color and his ability to craft complex and nuanced characters that defied traditional gender roles and stereotypes.

Abbas Kiarostami: From Iran came Abbas Kiarostami, whose films like Close-Up and Taste of Cherry explored themes such as identity, reality, and the nature of truth. Kiarostami was known for his use of minimalist techniques and his ability to blur the line between fiction and reality, as well as his focus on the lives of ordinary people and their struggles.

Ang Lee: Another major figure in global cinema during this period was Ang Lee, the Taiwanese-born director whose films like The Wedding Banquet and Crouching Tiger, Hidden Dragon explored themes such as cultural identity, tradition, and family. Lee was known for his ability to blend elements of both Eastern and Western cinema, as well as his use of stunning visuals and action sequences.

Conclusion: The filmmakers of this period were true innovators who pushed the boundaries of what was possible in global cinema. From Kurosawa's epic samurai films to Wong Kar-wai's poetic exploration of modern Hong Kong, these filmmakers crafted works that continue to inspire and captivate audiences to this day. In the next section, we will explore the impact of globalization on the film industry and how it helped to shape the emergence of global cinema during this period.

The impact of globalization on the film industry

Globalization, the process of increasing interconnectedness and interdependence between nations, had a profound impact on the film industry during the period of 1980-2000. In this section, we will explore the ways in which globalization influenced the production, distribution, and reception of films during this period, and how it helped to shape the emergence of global cinema as a distinct phenomenon.

The Rise of International Co-Productions: One of the most significant ways in which globalization impacted the film industry during this period was through the rise of international co-productions, in which films were produced with financial and creative contributions from multiple countries. This trend allowed filmmakers to access new sources of funding and expertise, and helped to facilitate the exchange of ideas and techniques across national boundaries.

The Impact of Hollywood on Global Cinema: Another key aspect of globalization in the film industry was the growing influence of Hollywood on global cinema. With the increasing dominance of American films in international markets, many filmmakers around the world sought to emulate Hollywood's style and production values in order to appeal to wider audiences. At the same time, however, this trend also led to concerns about the homogenization of global cinema and the erosion of cultural diversity.

The Emergence of New Markets: Globalization also created new opportunities for filmmakers to reach audiences in previously untapped markets around the world. With the growth of international film festivals and the proliferation of digital technologies, films from non-Western countries were able to reach a global audience in a way that was not possible before. This trend helped to elevate the status of filmmakers from regions like Latin America, Asia, and Africa, and helped to promote greater cultural exchange and understanding.

Challenges and Opportunities: While globalization brought many benefits to the film industry during this period, it also created new challenges and opportunities for filmmakers. With the increased competition and financial pressures that came with global markets, many filmmakers struggled to maintain their artistic integrity and vision, while others found new ways to experiment and innovate within the context of global cinema.

Conclusion: The impact of globalization on the film industry during the period of 1980-2000 was profound and far-reaching, shaping the emergence of global cinema as a distinct phenomenon that continues to evolve to this day.

From the rise of international co-productions to the challenges and opportunities presented by new markets, globalization had a profound impact on the way films were made, distributed, and received during this period. In the next section, we will explore the emergence of Latin American cinema and its impact on global cinema during this period.

Chapter 1: Hollywood and Beyond
The influence of Hollywood on global cinema

The influence of Hollywood on global cinema during the period of 1980-2000 was significant and far-reaching. With the rise of globalization and the increasing dominance of American films in international markets, many filmmakers around the world sought to emulate Hollywood's style and production values in order to appeal to wider audiences. In this section, we will explore the ways in which Hollywood influenced global cinema during this period, and the impact this had on the diversity and creativity of the film industry.

The Dominance of Hollywood: During the 1980s and 1990s, Hollywood dominated the global film industry, with American films accounting for a large share of box office revenue around the world. This dominance was driven by a range of factors, including the quality and popularity of American films, the strength of the American distribution and marketing infrastructure, and the increasing consolidation of the film industry under the control of large media conglomerates.

The Influence of Hollywood Style: One of the key ways in which Hollywood influenced global cinema during this period was through the dissemination of its distinctive style and production values. From the use of high-budget special effects to the emphasis on star power and marketing, Hollywood's influence on global cinema was evident in the films produced by many international filmmakers, who sought to emulate the glamour and sophistication of American movies.

The Challenge of Cultural Diversity: While Hollywood's influence on global cinema helped to promote the exchange of ideas and techniques across national boundaries, it also created challenges for filmmakers seeking to preserve and promote cultural diversity. With the homogenization of global cinema under the influence of Hollywood style and values, many filmmakers struggled to maintain their own artistic vision and cultural identity in the face of the pressures of global markets.

The Emergence of New Voices: Despite the challenges posed by Hollywood's dominance, the period of 1980-2000 also saw the emergence of new voices and perspectives within global cinema. Filmmakers from regions like Asia, Africa, and Latin America began to assert their own unique visions and styles, challenging the hegemony of Hollywood and promoting greater cultural diversity within the film industry.

Conclusion: The influence of Hollywood on global cinema during the period of 1980-2000 was profound and far-reaching, shaping the emergence of global cinema as a distinct phenomenon. From the dominance of American films in international markets to the dissemination of Hollywood style and values, Hollywood's impact on global cinema was significant. However, this influence also created challenges for filmmakers seeking to maintain their own artistic vision and cultural identity, and prompted a renewed focus on promoting greater diversity within the film industry. In the next section, we will explore the rise of international co-productions and their impact on global cinema.

The rise of international co-productions

During the period of 1980-2000, there was a significant increase in international co-productions between Hollywood and foreign film industries. These collaborations between countries allowed for a mix of talents, ideas, and resources, resulting in some of the most memorable and successful films of the era.

One of the earliest examples of an international co-production was "Raiders of the Lost Ark" (1981), directed by Steven Spielberg and produced by George Lucas. The film was a collaboration between Hollywood and British production companies, with much of the filming taking place in Tunisia. This co-production allowed for the incorporation of a diverse range of talents and resources, resulting in a highly successful film that appealed to audiences around the world.

Another notable example of international co-production is the French film "Betty Blue" (1986), directed by Jean-Jacques Beineix and produced by Claudie Ossard. The film was a collaboration between France and the United States, with the screenplay written in both French and English. The film's success in both countries highlighted the benefits of international co-productions, including access to larger audiences and greater financial resources.

The rise of international co-productions also had significant implications for the film industry as a whole. As more and more countries became involved in co-productions, the industry became more globalized, with new ideas and perspectives coming from all corners of the world. This globalization of the film industry allowed for greater diversity in storytelling and representation, as filmmakers from different backgrounds were able to share their experiences and perspectives.

However, international co-productions also presented challenges, including differences in language, culture, and production standards. Co-productions required careful negotiation and communication to ensure that all parties involved were satisfied with the final product. Additionally, some critics argued that international co-productions resulted in films that were too generic and lacked cultural specificity.

Despite these challenges, the rise of international co-productions during the period of 1980-2000 had a significant impact on the film industry, allowing for greater collaboration and diversity in storytelling. Today, international co-productions continue to be a vital part of the film industry, bringing together talents from around the world to create memorable and impactful films.

The impact of Hollywood on foreign language films

The impact of Hollywood on foreign language films is a complex and multifaceted subject. On the one hand, Hollywood has played a crucial role in popularizing foreign language films around the world, introducing audiences to new cultures and new styles of filmmaking. On the other hand, Hollywood's dominance of the global film market has also had a homogenizing effect, pushing many foreign language filmmakers to conform to Hollywood conventions in order to reach a wider audience.

One of the ways in which Hollywood has impacted foreign language films is through the distribution and exhibition of these films. In many countries, Hollywood studios control a large share of the screens in cinemas, which means that foreign language films often struggle to find an audience. This has led to the rise of alternative distribution channels, such as film festivals, art-house cinemas, and online platforms, which have helped to increase the visibility of foreign language films.

However, even when foreign language films do manage to secure a theatrical release, they often face a number of challenges. For one thing, many audiences are reluctant to watch films with subtitles, which can make it difficult for foreign language films to find an audience outside of their home countries. This has led some filmmakers to experiment with different approaches to subtitling, such as using voice-over narration or incorporating subtitles into the film's visual style.

Another way in which Hollywood has impacted foreign language films is through the influence of its storytelling conventions. Hollywood films often prioritize narrative clarity and emotional accessibility, which can lead to a preference for linear plots, clear-cut heroes and villains, and happy endings. This approach can be at odds with the more complex, ambiguous storytelling styles of many foreign language films.

Despite these challenges, however, foreign language films continue to thrive around the world, and many filmmakers have found ways to incorporate Hollywood conventions into their work without sacrificing their distinct cultural identity. Indeed, some of the most successful international co-productions have been the result of collaborations between Hollywood studios and foreign language filmmakers, such as the works of Ang Lee, Alejandro González Iñárritu, and Guillermo del Toro.

Overall, the impact of Hollywood on foreign language films is both positive and negative. While Hollywood's dominance of the global film market can be a barrier to entry for many foreign language filmmakers, it can also provide opportunities for collaboration and exposure to new audiences. As the film industry continues to evolve in the 21st century, it will be interesting to see how these dynamics continue to play out, and what new opportunities and challenges arise for foreign language filmmakers.

Chapter 2: The New Wave of Latin American Cinema

The emergence of Latin American cinema in the 80s and 90s

Latin American cinema has a rich and complex history, which can be traced back to the early 20th century. However, it was during the 1980s and 1990s that Latin American cinema experienced a new wave of creativity and innovation. This new wave was characterized by a renewed focus on social and political issues, as well as a growing interest in experimentation and hybridity.

One of the key factors that contributed to the emergence of the new wave of Latin American cinema was the changing political landscape of the region. During the 1980s and 1990s, many Latin American countries were undergoing a period of transition, as military dictatorships gave way to more democratic forms of government. This period of political transition created new opportunities for filmmakers to explore the social and political issues of the region.

Another important factor that contributed to the emergence of the new wave of Latin American cinema was the increasing availability of new technologies and funding opportunities. The advent of video technology and the growth of film festivals created new opportunities for independent filmmakers to produce and distribute their work.

One of the most important films of the new wave of Latin American cinema was "Tropico de Sangre" (1983) by Juan Bosch. The film tells the story of the Mirabal sisters, who were political activists in the Dominican Republic and were assassinated by the regime of Rafael Trujillo. The film was a critical and commercial success, and it helped to spark a renewed interest in Latin American cinema both within and outside the region.

Other important filmmakers of the new wave of Latin American cinema include Fernando Solanas, who directed the seminal film "The Hour of the Furnaces" (1968), and Hector Babenco, who directed "Kiss of the Spider Woman" (1985), which won the Palme d'Or at the Cannes Film Festival.

One of the defining features of the new wave of Latin American cinema was its focus on hybridity and experimentation. Many filmmakers began to blend elements of traditional Latin American culture with more contemporary forms of expression, creating works that were both innovative and deeply rooted in their cultural heritage.

For example, the Mexican filmmaker Guillermo del Toro created the film "Cronos" (1993), which combines elements of horror and fantasy with Mexican folklore. The film was a critical success and helped to establish del Toro as one of the most innovative filmmakers of his generation.

Overall, the emergence of the new wave of Latin American cinema in the 1980s and 1990s represented a significant shift in the region's cultural landscape. Through their innovative and socially engaged works, Latin American filmmakers were able to capture the complexity and diversity of their cultural heritage, while also exploring the pressing social and political issues of their time.

The major filmmakers and their works

The emergence of Latin American cinema in the 1980s and 1990s brought with it a group of visionary filmmakers who would go on to make some of the most groundbreaking and influential films of the era. In this chapter, we will explore some of the most important Latin American filmmakers of this period and the films that made them famous.

1. Fernando Solanas

Fernando Solanas is an Argentine film director, screenwriter, and politician, and is considered one of the founding members of the "Third Cinema" movement. He is best known for his films "The Hour of the Furnaces" (1968) and "Sur" (1988). "The Hour of the Furnaces" is a three-part documentary film that explores the history of Argentina and the struggles of the working class, while "Sur" is a poetic and personal reflection on Argentina's past and present.

2. Hector Babenco

Hector Babenco was a Brazilian film director and producer, best known for his films "Pixote" (1981) and "Kiss of the Spider Woman" (1985). "Pixote" is a gritty and realistic portrayal of street life in Brazil, while "Kiss of the Spider Woman" is a powerful and emotional story of two men who become unlikely friends while in prison.

3. Alejandro Jodorowsky

Alejandro Jodorowsky is a Chilean-French filmmaker and artist, known for his surrealist and avant-garde films. His most famous films include "El Topo" (1970) and "The Holy Mountain" (1973). "El Topo" is a violent and psychedelic Western, while "The Holy Mountain" is a surreal and symbolic journey through the Tarot.

4. Guillermo del Toro

Guillermo del Toro is a Mexican film director, screenwriter, and producer, known for his imaginative and visually stunning films. His most famous works include "Pan's Labyrinth" (2006) and "The Shape of Water" (2017). "Pan's Labyrinth" is a dark and fantastical story set during the Spanish Civil War, while "The Shape of Water" is a romantic fantasy about a woman who falls in love with a sea creature.

5. Lucrecia Martel

Lucrecia Martel is an Argentine film director, screenwriter, and producer, known for her unique and challenging films. Her most famous works include "La Cienaga" (2001) and "The Headless Woman" (2008). "La Cienaga" is a dark and humorous portrayal of a dysfunctional family, while "The Headless Woman" is a mysterious and unsettling story of a woman who may or may not have caused a car accident.

6. Glauber Rocha

Glauber Rocha was a Brazilian film director, screenwriter, and actor, and one of the key figures of the Cinema Novo movement. His most famous films include "Black God, White Devil" (1964) and "Antonio das Mortes" (1969). "Black God, White Devil" is a violent and poetic exploration of religion and revolution, while "Antonio das Mortes" is a surreal and existential Western.

7. Alfonso Arau

Alfonso Arau is a Mexican film director, screenwriter, and actor, known for his intimate and heartfelt films. His most famous works include "Like Water for Chocolate" (1992) and "A Walk in the Clouds" (1995). "Like Water for Chocolate" is a magical and sensual story set in a Mexican kitchen, while "A Walk in the Clouds" is a romantic drama set in a Napa Valley vineyard.

These filmmakers, and many others like them, contributed to the emergence of a distinct Latin American cinema in the 1980s and 1990s. This new wave of cinema explored the complexities of Latin American culture, its history, and its relationship with the rest of the world. These films often dealt with themes such as poverty, social injustice, and political upheaval. They were also characterized by a strong visual style, which reflected the vibrant and colorful nature of Latin American culture. As a result, Latin American cinema gained international recognition and became an important part of global cinema during this period.

The influence of political and social issues on Latin American cinema

Latin American cinema has been heavily influenced by the region's complex political and social issues. Many Latin American countries have faced political turmoil, social upheaval, and economic struggles throughout the 20th century, and these experiences have often found their way onto the screen. Latin American cinema has a rich tradition of using film to explore political and social issues, and to give voice to those who have been marginalized or oppressed.

One of the most significant political events in Latin America during the 20th century was the Cuban Revolution of 1959. The revolution brought Fidel Castro to power and established a communist government in Cuba. The revolution also inspired leftist movements throughout Latin America and led to a surge in political and social activism. Cuban filmmakers were among the first to embrace the new revolutionary spirit and to use film as a means of promoting social change. Films such as "Memories of Underdevelopment" (1968) and "Lucía" (1968) were critical of the pre-revolutionary status quo and celebrated the potential of the revolution to bring about positive change.

Other Latin American countries also experienced political turmoil during this period. In Chile, the socialist government of Salvador Allende was overthrown in a coup d'état in 1973, and a military dictatorship led by General Augusto Pinochet was established. The Pinochet regime was characterized by brutal repression and human rights abuses, and Chilean filmmakers responded with a wave of political films that exposed the regime's crimes and called for an end to the dictatorship. Films such as "The Battle of Chile" (1975-1979), "Missing" (1982), and "No" (2012) are powerful indictments of the Pinochet regime and a testament to the resilience of the Chilean people in the face of oppression.

In Brazil, the military dictatorship that ruled the country from 1964 to 1985 also inspired a wave of politically engaged filmmaking. The Cinema Novo movement, which emerged in the 1960s, sought to create a new kind of Brazilian cinema that was rooted in the country's social realities and that challenged the dominant narrative of Brazil as a land of sunshine, samba, and soccer. Films such as "Black God, White Devil" (1964) and "The Hour of the Star" (1985) explored issues of poverty, inequality, and oppression in Brazil and helped to establish Brazil as a major player in the world of cinema.

In addition to political issues, Latin American cinema has also addressed a wide range of social issues. Films have explored topics such as poverty, gender roles, and the role of the Catholic Church in society. One of the most significant social issues in Latin America is the marginalization of indigenous peoples, who often suffer discrimination and oppression at the hands of the dominant culture. Films such as "Yawar Mallku" (1969) and "Babel" (2006) have explored the experiences of indigenous peoples and challenged the dominant cultural narrative.

Overall, the influence of political and social issues on Latin American cinema has been profound. Latin American filmmakers have used their art to give voice to the voiceless, to promote social change, and to challenge the dominant cultural narrative. Through their work, they have established Latin American cinema as a powerful force in the world of film, and have helped to create a more nuanced and complex understanding of the region and its people.

Chapter 3: The Rise of African Cinema

The emergence of African cinema during this period

The emergence of African cinema during the period of 1980-2000 was a significant development in the global film industry. The rise of African cinema was closely tied to the continent's history and the socio-political changes that occurred during this period. In the 1980s and 1990s, many African countries gained independence from colonial rule and underwent significant transformations. This led to a growing desire for cultural expression and the emergence of a new generation of African filmmakers.

One of the earliest and most prominent figures of African cinema during this period was Ousmane Sembène, a Senegalese film director and writer. Sembène's films were known for their social commentary and exploration of themes related to colonialism, racism, and class struggle. His films "Black Girl" (1966), "Xala" (1975), and "Camp de Thiaroye" (1988) were critically acclaimed and widely influential in shaping the direction of African cinema.

Another notable figure in African cinema during this period was Djibril Diop Mambéty, also from Senegal. Mambéty's films were characterized by their surrealism and allegorical storytelling. His films "Touki Bouki" (1973) and "Hyenas" (1992) were landmarks of African cinema, exploring themes related to post-colonial identity and cultural hybridity.

In addition to these filmmakers, other African countries also began to produce their own films during this period. In Nigeria, for example, a film industry known as Nollywood emerged and quickly became one of the largest film industries in the world. Nollywood films were known for their low budgets and rapid production schedules, but they also tackled important social and political issues facing Nigeria and Africa as a whole.

Overall, the emergence of African cinema during the period of 1980-2000 was a significant development that reflected the changing political and social landscape of the continent. African filmmakers used cinema as a means of expressing their cultural identity and exploring important issues related to colonialism, racism, and socio-economic inequality.

The major filmmakers and their works

The emergence of African cinema in the 1980s and 1990s brought about a new wave of filmmakers who told stories that were previously overlooked or ignored by the mainstream. These filmmakers used their art as a means of challenging the social, political and economic status quo. Some of the most significant filmmakers and their works during this period include:

1. Ousmane Sembene - Known as the "father of African cinema," Sembene is a Senegalese writer and filmmaker who gained international recognition with his films, "Black Girl" (1966), "Mandabi" (1968), and "Xala" (1975). His work is known for its criticism of post-colonial African societies and the impact of colonialism.

2. Djibril Diop Mambety - A Senegalese film director, actor, and composer, Mambety is best known for his film "Hyenas" (1992), which is a biting critique of post-colonial African society. His films are characterized by a blend of satire, humor, and social commentary.

3. Souleymane Cissé - A Malian filmmaker, Cissé is known for his films "Brightness" (1987) and "Waati" (1995). His films often explore themes of African identity, colonialism, and the impact of modernization on traditional societies.

4. Idrissa Ouedraogo - A Burkinabe filmmaker, Ouedraogo is known for his films "Tilai" (1990) and "Samba Traoré" (1992). His films often explore themes of tradition versus modernity, political corruption, and the challenges of African youth.

5. Mahamat Saleh Haroun - A Chadian filmmaker, Haroun gained international recognition with his film "Daratt" (2006). His films often explore themes of displacement, war, and the complexities of African identity.

These filmmakers, and many others like them, were instrumental in shaping African cinema during this period. Their works paved the way for a new generation of filmmakers to tell their stories and challenge the dominant narratives about Africa and its people.

The influence of post-colonialism on African cinema

The emergence of African cinema in the 1980s and 1990s was strongly influenced by post-colonialism, as many African nations had recently gained their independence from European colonial powers. This new wave of cinema represented a departure from earlier films that had largely been produced by colonial powers for the purpose of promoting their own interests.

Post-colonial African cinema often focused on issues related to identity, culture, and politics. Many of these films sought to challenge prevailing stereotypes of Africa and Africans that had been perpetuated by Western media. They also explored themes of national liberation, social justice, and cultural affirmation.

One of the most prominent figures in post-colonial African cinema was Ousmane Sembène, a Senegalese filmmaker who is often referred to as the "father of African cinema." Sembène's films, such as "Black Girl" (1966) and "Xala" (1975), explored the impact of colonialism and the struggle for independence in Africa. His work also explored issues of gender, class, and cultural identity in African societies.

Another notable filmmaker was Djibril Diop Mambéty, a Senegalese director who is best known for his film "Hyenas" (1992). Like Sembène, Mambéty's work often dealt with themes of colonialism, national identity, and social justice. His films were known for their surreal and allegorical elements, which he used to critique post-colonial African societies.

Other notable post-colonial African filmmakers include Gaston Kaboré of Burkina Faso, whose film "Wend Kuuni" (1982) explored the role of traditional African beliefs in contemporary society, and Mahamat Saleh Haroun of Chad, whose film "Daratt" (2006) dealt with the legacy of violence in post-colonial African societies.

Post-colonialism continues to be a major influence on African cinema to this day, as filmmakers grapple with issues related to globalization, neo-colonialism, and cultural preservation. The legacy of post-colonial African cinema has had a profound impact on the wider world of cinema, influencing filmmakers and audiences alike with its unique perspectives and powerful storytelling.

Chapter 4: The Asian New Wave
The emergence of Asian cinema in the late 90s

The late 90s saw the emergence of a new wave of Asian cinema, marked by a fresh perspective and innovative techniques. This new wave drew upon both traditional and modern themes, and was characterized by a daring and experimental approach to storytelling. One of the key factors driving this wave was the globalization of the film industry, which allowed Asian filmmakers to reach a wider audience than ever before.

One of the most influential films of the Asian new wave was Wong Kar-wai's "Chungking Express" (1994). This film, which tells the story of two lovelorn police officers in Hong Kong, features Wong's signature visual style, with its lush colors and stylized camerawork. "Chungking Express" was a commercial and critical success, and is often cited as a seminal work of the Asian new wave.

Another important film of the Asian new wave was Takeshi Kitano's "Hana-bi" (1997). Kitano, a Japanese actor and director, had already established himself as a major talent with films like "Sonatine" (1993) and "Violent Cop" (1989). But "Hana-bi" marked a new phase in his career, with its mix of violence, humor, and sentimentality. The film won the Golden Lion at the Venice Film Festival, and cemented Kitano's reputation as one of Asia's most innovative directors.

Other notable films of the Asian new wave include Zhang Yimou's "Raise the Red Lantern" (1991), which explores the lives of concubines in a wealthy Chinese household, and Park Chan-wook's "Oldboy" (2003), a brutal revenge thriller that won the Grand Prix at the Cannes Film Festival. These films, and many others like them, pushed the boundaries of what was possible in Asian cinema, and helped to establish a new generation of filmmakers with a unique voice and vision.

Overall, the emergence of the Asian new wave in the late 90s marked a significant moment in the history of global cinema. These films demonstrated the diversity and creativity of Asian filmmaking, and paved the way for a new era of international recognition and acclaim.

The major filmmakers and their works

The Asian New Wave produced some of the most iconic films in global cinema, introducing the world to a new generation of filmmakers who were determined to push the boundaries of their craft. Here are some of the major filmmakers and their works that emerged during this period:

1. Wong Kar-wai - Hong Kong Wong Kar-wai is considered one of the greatest filmmakers of his generation, known for his unique and visually stunning films. His most famous works include "Chungking Express" (1994), "In the Mood for Love" (2000), and "2046" (2004). His films often explore themes of love, loss, and memory, and his use of vibrant colors and stylized cinematography has had a lasting influence on the film industry.

2. Hayao Miyazaki - Japan Hayao Miyazaki is a legendary Japanese animator, filmmaker, and co-founder of the famed Studio Ghibli. His most famous works include "Spirited Away" (2001), "Princess Mononoke" (1997), and "My Neighbor Totoro" (1988). His films often feature strong environmental themes and explore the relationship between humans and nature.

3. Park Chan-wook - South Korea Park Chan-wook is a South Korean filmmaker known for his violent and visually striking films. His most famous works include "Oldboy"

(2003), "Lady Vengeance" (2005), and "The Handmaiden" (2016). His films often explore themes of revenge, justice, and morality, and his use of intricate camera work and striking visuals has made him a major influence in modern cinema.

4. Zhang Yimou - China Zhang Yimou is a Chinese filmmaker known for his visually stunning and emotionally complex films. His most famous works include "Raise the Red Lantern" (1991), "Hero" (2002), and "House of Flying Daggers" (2004). His films often explore themes of power, politics, and the human condition, and his use of color and composition has made him a major influence in world cinema.

5. Apichatpong Weerasethakul - Thailand Apichatpong Weerasethakul is a Thai filmmaker known for his dreamlike and surreal films. His most famous works include "Uncle Boonmee Who Can Recall His Past Lives" (2010), "Syndromes and a Century" (2006), and "Cemetery of Splendor" (2015). His films often explore themes of memory, identity, and the supernatural, and his unique approach to storytelling and cinematic style has made him a major figure in modern cinema.

These filmmakers, along with many others, helped shape the Asian New Wave and brought a fresh perspective to the film industry. Their unique visions and storytelling techniques have had a lasting impact on global cinema and continue to inspire filmmakers around the world.

The influence of globalization on Asian cinema

The Asian New Wave emerged in the late 1990s as a response to the growing global interest in Asian cinema. With the increase in global trade and the spread of technology, Asian cinema was no longer confined to local audiences and began to gain international recognition. The emergence of this new wave was also influenced by the economic and political changes that took place in Asia during this period.

One of the main features of the Asian New Wave was the use of new technologies and the adoption of a more global approach to filmmaking. This was reflected in the use of new digital technologies, such as computer-generated imagery, that allowed Asian filmmakers to produce high-quality films on a smaller budget. Additionally, the use of more international themes and stories, as well as collaborations with foreign actors and producers, helped Asian films to reach a wider audience.

Some of the major filmmakers of the Asian New Wave include Wong Kar-wai, Park Chan-wook, and Hou Hsiao-hsien. Wong Kar-wai is a Hong Kong filmmaker known for his stylized and visually stunning films, such as "Chungking Express" (1994) and "In the Mood for Love" (2000). Park Chan-wook is a South Korean filmmaker known for his violent and psychologically complex films, such as "Oldboy" (2003) and "Thirst" (2009). Hou Hsiao-hsien is a Taiwanese filmmaker known for his minimalist and contemplative style, as seen in his films "The Puppetmaster" (1993) and "Three Times" (2005).

These filmmakers and others like them helped to establish the Asian New Wave as a significant force in global cinema, as their films often reflected the unique cultural perspectives of Asia while also appealing to international audiences. The Asian New Wave also paved the way for other Asian filmmakers to gain recognition and explore new artistic and thematic territories.

Furthermore, the impact of globalization on Asian cinema was significant during this period. The rise of globalization led to the integration of the Asian film industry with the global market. As a result, Asian filmmakers were able to tap into a wider range of resources, including funding, distribution channels, and marketing strategies. This allowed for greater exposure and success for Asian films in international markets.

However, the influence of globalization also brought challenges for Asian cinema, such as the potential loss of cultural identity and authenticity in films. Many Asian filmmakers were pressured to conform to Western standards of filmmaking and storytelling in order to appeal to a global audience. This led to debates about the balance between cultural authenticity and international appeal, and how to navigate the challenges of a global film industry while still maintaining cultural roots.

In conclusion, the emergence of the Asian New Wave in the late 1990s brought significant changes to Asian cinema, with the use of new technologies and a more global approach to filmmaking. The major filmmakers of the Asian New Wave, such as Wong Kar-wai, Park Chan-wook, and Hou Hsiao-hsien, helped to establish Asia as a significant force in global cinema. The influence of globalization on Asian cinema during this period also brought both opportunities and challenges for Asian filmmakers, highlighting the need to balance cultural authenticity with global appeal.

Chapter 5: European Cinema in Transition
The evolution of European cinema during this period

The period of 1980-2000 saw a significant evolution in European cinema. With the rise of independent and arthouse cinema, European filmmakers explored new themes and styles, often pushing the boundaries of conventional storytelling.

One of the major changes in European cinema during this period was the decline of national cinema industries and the rise of transnational cinema. As countries began to open up their markets to foreign films, European cinema faced stiff competition from Hollywood and other global film industries. In response, many European filmmakers began to collaborate with international partners and produce co-productions, resulting in films that transcended national borders and explored universal themes.

Another significant trend in European cinema during this period was the rise of arthouse and independent cinema. Filmmakers such as Lars von Trier, Pedro Almodovar, and Michael Haneke gained international acclaim for their innovative and daring films. These filmmakers challenged traditional cinematic conventions, experimenting with non-linear storytelling, ambiguous narratives, and unconventional editing techniques.

In addition, many European filmmakers explored complex social and political issues during this period. For example, the collapse of the Soviet Union and the end of the Cold War led to a new focus on issues such as immigration, globalization, and cultural identity. Films such as Mathieu Kassovitz's "La Haine" (1995) explored the lives of young people in the Parisian suburbs, while Ken Loach's "Raining Stones" (1993) examined the impact of unemployment on working-class families in England.

Overall, the evolution of European cinema during the period of 1980-2000 reflected a shift towards transnationalism, arthouse and independent cinema, and a focus on complex social and political issues. European filmmakers pushed the boundaries of conventional storytelling, exploring new themes and styles that challenged traditional cinematic norms.

European cinema has a long and illustrious history, with a diverse range of filmmakers and styles. During the 1980s and 1990s, European cinema was in a period of transition, as filmmakers sought to find new ways of telling stories and engaging audiences. Some of the most important European filmmakers during this period include:

1. Pedro Almodóvar Pedro Almodóvar is a Spanish filmmaker known for his colorful and flamboyant style. His films often explore themes of sexuality, gender, and identity, and are celebrated for their vivid visual style and complex storytelling. Some of his most famous works include "Women on the Verge of a Nervous Breakdown" (1988), "All About My Mother" (1999), and "Talk to Her" (2002).

2. Lars von Trier Lars von Trier is a Danish filmmaker known for his provocative and controversial films. His works often challenge conventional cinematic norms and explore difficult and uncomfortable subject matter. Some of his most famous films include "Breaking the Waves" (1996), "Dancer in the Dark" (2000), and "Melancholia" (2011).

3. Jean-Pierre Jeunet Jean-Pierre Jeunet is a French filmmaker known for his whimsical and fantastical films. His works often feature intricate visual effects and elaborate set designs, and are characterized by their quirky and charming

characters. Some of his most famous films include "Amélie" (2001), "A Very Long Engagement" (2004), and "Micmacs" (2009).

4. Krzysztof Kieślowski Krzysztof Kieślowski was a Polish filmmaker known for his poetic and philosophical approach to cinema. His films often explore themes of morality, destiny, and human nature, and are celebrated for their beautiful cinematography and complex storytelling. Some of his most famous works include "The Double Life of Veronique" (1991) and the "Three Colors" trilogy (1993-1994).

5. Michael Haneke Michael Haneke is an Austrian filmmaker known for his dark and unsettling films. His works often explore themes of violence, alienation, and existentialism, and are celebrated for their uncompromising and challenging approach to storytelling. Some of his most famous films include "Funny Games" (1997), "The Piano Teacher" (2001), and "Amour" (2012).

These filmmakers, along with many others, played an important role in shaping European cinema during the 1980s and 1990s. They experimented with new styles and techniques, challenged cinematic norms, and created some of the most innovative and exciting films of the period. Their works continue to influence and inspire filmmakers around the world.

The influence of globalization on European cinema

Globalization has had a significant impact on the film industry, and European cinema has not been immune to its effects. The rise of Hollywood and the increasing dominance of American cinema have had a profound influence on European cinema, leading to changes in both the production and distribution of films. In this section, we will examine the ways in which globalization has affected European cinema.

One of the most significant effects of globalization on European cinema has been the rise of international co-productions. As production costs have increased, many European filmmakers have turned to co-productions with other countries to finance their films. These co-productions often involve collaborations with American studios, as well as with other European countries. Co-productions allow filmmakers to access larger budgets, better production facilities, and more extensive distribution networks, but they also mean that films must be designed to appeal to a wider international audience.

Another impact of globalization has been the increasing homogenization of European cinema. Many European films now share the same production values and visual styles as Hollywood films. This is partly due to the influence of American filmmakers and studios on European filmmakers, but it is also a response to the demands of the global marketplace. European films are increasingly designed to be easily exportable to other countries, which means that they often feature recognizable genres, characters, and themes that are familiar to international audiences.

The distribution of European films has also been affected by globalization. The increasing dominance of American distributors and exhibitors has made it harder for European films to find a global audience. Many European films are now released in only a handful of cinemas outside of their home countries, and even those that do receive wider distribution often struggle to compete with Hollywood blockbusters. This has led to a growing concern about the impact of globalization on European cultural identity, with many filmmakers and cultural commentators arguing that European cinema is in danger of losing its distinctive character and voice.

Despite these challenges, however, European cinema continues to thrive. The rise of digital technology has made it easier and cheaper for filmmakers to produce and distribute their films, and the growing popularity of streaming services has provided new opportunities for European films to reach a global audience. Moreover, many European filmmakers are now embracing the challenges and opportunities presented by globalization, seeking to create films that are both commercially viable and artistically innovative. As such, European cinema remains an important and dynamic part of the global film industry.

Chapter 6: The Future of Global Cinema
The current state of global cinema

The film industry has undergone significant changes in recent years due to the rapid advancements in technology and the increasing global interconnectedness. The traditional film distribution models have given way to new digital platforms and streaming services, which have altered the way audiences consume films. Additionally, there has been a rise in international co-productions and collaborations, resulting in a more diverse and globalized cinema.

One of the most significant developments in recent years is the emergence of streaming services, which have disrupted the traditional theatrical release model. Services like Netflix, Amazon Prime Video, and Disney+ have become major players in the film industry, producing and distributing films that would have otherwise struggled to find a theatrical release. These platforms have given filmmakers greater creative freedom, as they are not bound by the constraints of a theatrical release, and have also provided audiences with greater access to a wider range of films.

Another trend that has emerged is the rise of international co-productions and collaborations. As the world becomes more connected, filmmakers from different countries are collaborating on projects, resulting in films that reflect a more diverse range of perspectives and experiences. The success of films like "Parasite" (2019) and "Roma" (2018) demonstrates the growing appetite for these types of films, which have resonated with audiences worldwide.

Despite these changes, traditional cinema remains an important part of the film industry. While the pandemic has resulted in widespread theater closures and disruptions, many people still value the communal experience of watching a film on the big screen. Furthermore, some filmmakers still view the theatrical release as the optimal way to showcase their work, and many films continue to receive critical acclaim and commercial success through traditional theatrical releases.

Overall, the current state of global cinema is one that is rapidly evolving and adapting to the changing landscape. While the industry faces many challenges, such as the ongoing impact of the pandemic and the struggle to balance artistic vision with commercial viability, there is a sense of excitement and potential for the future of cinema. As technology continues to advance and the world becomes more connected, the possibilities for global cinema are endless.

The challenges facing global cinema in the 21st century

The 21st century has brought about numerous challenges for global cinema. While the digital age has made it easier for filmmakers to produce and distribute their work, it has also created an oversaturated market, making it difficult for smaller and independent films to gain recognition. Additionally, changing audience preferences and the rise of streaming platforms have disrupted traditional distribution models, leading to a shift in the way films are consumed.

One of the major challenges facing global cinema is the lack of diversity in Hollywood and the dominance of Western narratives in mainstream cinema. This has led to a lack of representation for non-Western cultures and a limited understanding of the world outside of Hollywood's lens. However, the rise of international co-productions and the success of films like Parasite (2019) have shown that audiences are hungry for diverse stories and perspectives.

Another challenge is the impact of piracy on the film industry. The ease of accessing films online has made it difficult for filmmakers to earn a living from their work, as well as undermining the financial viability of the industry as a whole. Piracy has also created a lack of trust between filmmakers and audiences, as filmmakers may be hesitant to share their work for fear of it being stolen and distributed illegally.

The increasing cost of producing films is another challenge for global cinema. The rise of digital technology has made it easier for filmmakers to create visually stunning films, but it has also led to an increase in production costs. Additionally, the COVID-19 pandemic has brought about new challenges, such as restrictions on travel and large gatherings, making it difficult for filmmakers to produce films and for audiences to enjoy them in cinemas.

The shifting landscape of film distribution has also posed challenges for global cinema. With the rise of streaming platforms like Netflix and Amazon Prime, traditional theatrical releases are becoming less important. This has led to a decline in the number of cinemas, particularly in smaller towns and cities, and a shift in the way audiences consume films.

In conclusion, global cinema faces numerous challenges in the 21st century. However, the industry has shown resilience and adaptability in the face of these challenges, with filmmakers experimenting with new distribution models and technologies to reach audiences. As the world becomes more connected, it is important for the film industry to continue to push for diversity and representation, while also finding ways to sustainably produce and distribute films for a global audience.

The potential for global cinema in the future

The potential for global cinema in the future is vast, as technology and globalization continue to shape the industry. Here are some potential areas for growth:

1. Virtual Reality: Virtual reality technology has the potential to revolutionize cinema by offering viewers an immersive experience. Some filmmakers have already begun experimenting with VR, creating short films that transport viewers to different environments. As VR technology becomes more accessible and affordable, it could become a new form of storytelling that is more interactive and engaging than traditional cinema.

2. Streaming Services: The rise of streaming services like Netflix and Amazon Prime has changed the way people consume media. This has allowed for more diverse and niche content to be produced and distributed, as well as giving global filmmakers a wider audience. Streaming services have also increased the demand for foreign-language content, as viewers become more interested in exploring different cultures through cinema.

3. Co-Productions: Co-productions between countries have been on the rise, as filmmakers seek to collaborate and share resources. This can help bridge cultural gaps and bring different perspectives to the screen. As co-productions

become more common, they have the potential to create new forms of storytelling that are truly global in nature.

4. Diversity and Inclusion: The push for diversity and inclusion in the film industry has gained momentum in recent years, with more filmmakers from underrepresented groups being given opportunities to tell their stories. As the world becomes more interconnected, it is important for cinema to reflect the diversity of our society. By promoting diversity and inclusion, global cinema has the potential to reach new heights and bring people together through the power of storytelling.

5. Emerging Markets: As economies grow and develop around the world, new markets for cinema are emerging. Countries like China, India, and Brazil have become major players in the global film industry, both in terms of production and box office revenue. As these markets continue to expand, they will offer new opportunities for global filmmakers to share their stories with a wider audience.

In conclusion, the future of global cinema is bright, with potential for new forms of storytelling, increased diversity and inclusion, and a growing global audience. As technology and globalization continue to shape the industry, it is important for filmmakers to embrace new opportunities and explore new ways of telling stories that reflect the diverse perspectives of our world.

Conclusion
The significance of global cinema during the period of 1980-2000

The period of 1980-2000 was a crucial time for the development and growth of global cinema. During this period, the film industry underwent significant changes, with the rise of new waves of cinema from various parts of the world. This led to the emergence of a diverse range of voices and stories from different cultural contexts, challenging the dominance of Hollywood and western cinema. The impact of these changes can still be felt in contemporary cinema, with many of the innovations and trends that emerged during this period continuing to influence and shape global film culture.

One of the most significant developments of this period was the emergence of new voices from regions that had previously been marginalized in the film industry. Latin America, Africa, Asia, and Europe all experienced a new wave of cinema during this time, with filmmakers exploring themes and stories that were specific to their respective cultural contexts. This led to the creation of a diverse range of films, ranging from intimate character studies to epic historical dramas, all of which spoke to the particular experiences and perspectives of their creators.

At the same time, the rise of global cinema during this period also challenged traditional notions of film production, distribution, and consumption. With the growth of digital technologies, it became easier for filmmakers to create and distribute their work, leading to the emergence of new forms of independent and alternative cinema. This, in turn, challenged the dominance of the major studios and distribution networks, creating a more diverse and democratic film culture.

Moreover, the impact of globalization on the film industry also played a significant role during this period. With the growth of multinational corporations and the increasing interconnectedness of the global economy, cinema became more transnational, with films and filmmakers crossing borders and cultures. This led to the creation of new hybrid forms of cinema, with filmmakers blending different cultural and aesthetic traditions to create works that were uniquely global.

Looking back on this period, it is clear that global cinema played a significant role in shaping the cultural and political landscape of the late 20th century. The emergence of new voices and stories from previously marginalized regions challenged the dominance of Hollywood and western cinema, creating a more diverse and inclusive film culture. At the same time, the growth of digital technologies and the impact of globalization created new opportunities and challenges for filmmakers, leading to the creation of new forms of cinema that were more democratic and transnational in nature.

Today, the legacy of this period continues to influence and shape global cinema. Filmmakers from around the world continue to explore themes and stories that are specific to their cultural contexts, challenging traditional notions of film production and distribution. Moreover, the impact of digital technologies and globalization has only intensified in recent years, with new platforms and networks emerging that have the potential to transform the film industry even further. As such, it is clear that the significance of global cinema during the period of 1980-2000 cannot be overstated, and its legacy will continue to shape the film industry for years to come.

The lasting impact of the films and filmmakers of this period

The period of 1980-2000 was a significant time in the history of global cinema, marked by the emergence of new waves of filmmakers from Latin America, Africa, Asia, and Europe. These filmmakers brought new perspectives and styles, challenging the dominance of Hollywood and Western European cinema. In this concluding chapter, we will explore the lasting impact of the films and filmmakers of this period on global cinema.

One of the most significant contributions of the filmmakers of this period was the diversity of voices and perspectives they brought to the table. They explored issues such as post-colonialism, identity, globalization, and social inequality, among others, with a fresh and unique perspective. They challenged dominant narratives and provided an alternative vision of the world, paving the way for a more inclusive and diverse cinema.

The films of this period also introduced new aesthetics and narrative styles, pushing the boundaries of cinematic language. The use of handheld cameras, non-linear narratives, and unconventional editing techniques became more prevalent, giving rise to a new visual language that would influence generations of filmmakers to come. The films of Wong Kar-wai, Alejandro González Iñárritu, and Hou Hsiao-hsien, among others, are still celebrated for their innovative use of cinematography, sound design, and editing.

Furthermore, the films of this period had a significant impact on the film industry, both locally and globally. They proved that cinema could be both commercially successful and artistically ambitious, paving the way for a new generation of filmmakers who sought to break free from the constraints of mainstream cinema. The success of films like Crouching Tiger, Hidden Dragon, Amélie, and City of God demonstrated that there was a global audience for films that challenged the status quo, inspiring filmmakers from all over the world to push boundaries and explore new territory.

The lasting impact of the films and filmmakers of this period can also be seen in the current state of global cinema. The themes and issues explored in the films of this period continue to be relevant, and their influence can be felt in contemporary cinema. The use of handheld cameras and non-linear narratives, for instance, have become more commonplace in mainstream cinema, while the focus on diversity and representation has become a hot-button issue in the film industry.

In conclusion, the period of 1980-2000 was a significant time in the history of global cinema, marked by the emergence of new waves of filmmakers who challenged the status quo and introduced new perspectives and styles. Their films continue to inspire and influence filmmakers today, proving that cinema can be a powerful tool for social change and artistic expression. The films and filmmakers of this period have left an indelible mark on global cinema, shaping the way we see and understand the world around us.

The potential for global cinema in the future

Global cinema has come a long way since the 1980s and 1990s, and its potential for the future is immense. One of the key factors in this potential is the growth of technology, which has enabled filmmakers to create new, exciting, and innovative works. Digital filmmaking has made it easier for filmmakers to create high-quality films at lower costs, making it possible for more diverse voices to be heard.

Another factor is the growing interest in international film festivals and markets, which have opened up new opportunities for filmmakers to showcase their work and reach new audiences. With the rise of streaming platforms like Netflix and Amazon, there is an even greater potential for global cinema to reach wider audiences than ever before.

Furthermore, the increasing globalization of our world has created a greater interest in the stories and cultures of people from all over the world. As more people travel, study, and work in different countries, the demand for films that reflect diverse experiences and perspectives will continue to grow.

However, there are also challenges that global cinema will have to overcome to fully realize its potential. One of the biggest challenges is the dominance of Hollywood and Western media in the global market, which makes it difficult for non-Western films to compete. To overcome this, there needs to be greater support for local and independent cinema, as well as greater investment in film infrastructure and education.

Another challenge is the preservation of diverse film cultures and histories. As the film industry continues to evolve, it is important to remember and honor the rich and varied histories of global cinema. This can be done through film archives, preservation initiatives, and education programs that celebrate and promote the diversity of film cultures around the world.

In conclusion, the potential for global cinema in the future is immense, but it will require continued effort and investment to fully realize it. With the growth of technology, the increasing interest in international film festivals and markets, and the growing globalization of our world, there is a great opportunity for diverse and innovative films to reach wider audiences than ever before. However, there are also challenges that need to be addressed, including the dominance of Hollywood and Western media, and the preservation of diverse film cultures and histories. By addressing these challenges and supporting global cinema, we can create a more vibrant and inclusive film industry for generations to come.

THE END

Key Terms and Definitions

To help you better understand the language and concepts related to aging and older adults, below you will find a list of key terms and their definitions.

1. Global cinema: Refers to the collective body of films produced and exhibited worldwide, regardless of their country of origin.

2. New wave: A term used to describe a group of filmmakers who challenged traditional cinematic conventions and explored new techniques and styles.

3. Post-colonialism: A critical theory that examines the impact of colonialism on cultures and societies, and the ongoing effects of imperialism in the post-colonial era.

4. Globalization: The process of increasing interconnectedness and interdependence of economies, societies, and cultures across the world.

5. Transnational cinema: Refers to films that are produced in one country, but have transnational themes, characters, or settings, and are intended for a global audience.

6. Auteur: A term used to describe a filmmaker who has a distinctive style and vision, and exercises significant creative control over their films.

7. Art cinema: A type of filmmaking that emphasizes artistic expression and experimentation over commercial appeal, often characterized by complex narratives, ambiguous themes, and unconventional storytelling techniques.

8. Blockbuster: A term used to describe a commercially successful film that appeals to a wide audience and generates significant revenue.

9. Independent cinema: Refers to films that are produced outside of the major studio system, often with a lower budget and a focus on artistic expression and original storytelling.

10. Film festival: A public exhibition of films, often organized around a specific theme or genre, and featuring screenings, premieres, and discussions with filmmakers and critics.

Supporting Materials

Introduction:

- Bordwell, D. (2002). Film futures. Harvard University Press.

Chapter 1: Hollywood and Beyond

- Thompson, K. (2017). Film history: An introduction. McGraw-Hill Education.

- Klinger, B. (2006). Beyond the multiplex: Cinema, new technologies, and the home. University of California Press.

Chapter 2: The New Wave of Latin American Cinema

- King, J. (2014). New cinemas in Latin America. Bloomsbury Publishing.

- Martin, M. T. (2003). New Latin American cinema: Theory, practices, and transcontinental articulations. Wayne State University Press.

Chapter 3: The Rise of African Cinema

- Ukadike, N. F. (1994). Black African cinema. University of California Press.

- Gugler, J. (2016). African film: Looking back and looking forward. Indiana University Press.

Chapter 4: The Asian New Wave

- Marchetti, G. (2006). From Tian'anmen to Times Square: Transnational China and the Chinese diaspora on global screens, 1989-1997. Temple University Press.

- Wimal Dissanayake, W. (2003). Melodrama and Asian cinema. Cambridge University Press.

Chapter 5: European Cinema in Transition

- Elsaesser, T. (2015). European cinema and continental philosophy: Film as thought experiment. Bloomsbury Publishing.

- Hjort, M., & Petrie, D. (Eds.). (2007). The cinema of small nations. University of Edinburgh Press.

Chapter 6: The Future of Global Cinema

- Shohat, E. (2013). Taboo memories, diasporic voices. Duke University Press.

- Naficy, H. (2011). An accented cinema: Exilic and diasporic filmmaking. Princeton University Press.

Conclusion:

- Higson, A. (2003). English heritage, global cinema. Oxford University Press.

- Grewal, I., & Kaplan, C. (Eds.). (2001). An introduction to women's studies: Gender in a transnational world. McGraw-Hill.